Biomes
of North
America

A Walk
in the
Desert

by Rebecca L. Johnson

with illustrations by Phyllis V. Saroff

 CAROLRHODA BOOKS, INC./MINNEAPOLIS

*For my niece Claire, who helps me see
the world with fresh eyes*
—*R. L. J.*

Text copyright © 2001 by Rebecca L. Johnson
Illustrations copyright © 2001 by Phyllis V. Saroff

Map on p. 8 by Laura Westlund © 2001 by Carolrhoda Books, Inc.

Carolrhoda Books, Inc.
A division of Lerner Publishing Group
241 First Avenue North
Minneapolis, MN 55401 U.S.A.

Website address: www.lernerbooks.com

Library of Congress Cataloging-in-Publication Data

Johnson, Rebecca L.
   A walk in the desert / by Rebecca L. Johnson; illustrations by
Phyllis V. Saroff.
   p. cm. — (Biomes of North America)
   Includes index.
   Summary: Describes the climate, soil, plants, and animals of North
American deserts and the ways in which the plants and animals
depend on each other and their environment to survive.
   ISBN-13: 978-1-57505-152-9 (lib. bdg. : alk. paper)
   ISBN-10: 1-57505-152-4 (lib. bdg. : alk. paper)
1. Desert ecology—Juvenile literature. 2. Deserts—Juvenile literature.
[1. Desert ecology. 2. Deserts. 3. Ecology.] I. Saroff, Phyllis V., ill. II.
Title. III. Series: Johnson, Rebecca L. Biomes of North America.
QH541.5.D4 J65 2001   00-008251
577.54—dc21

Manufactured in the United States of America
6 7 8 9 10 11 - JR - 10 09 08 07 06 05

Words
to Know

BIOME (BYE-ohm)—a major community of living things that covers a large area, such as a grassland or a forest

CACTUS—a type of plant that usually grows in hot, dry places. Most cactus plants, or cacti, have thick stems that can store water. Cacti usually have sharp spines instead of leaves.

CLIMATE (KLYE-mut)—a region's usual pattern of weather over a long period of time

DESERT—a very dry region with rocky or sandy soil. Most deserts are very hot.

NECTAR—a sweet liquid produced by flowers. Nectar is used as food by animals such as bees, hummingbirds, and bats.

NOCTURNAL (nahk-TUR-nuhl)—active at night

POLLEN (PAH-luhn)—fine, powdery material made by flowers. Pollen is usually yellow.

PREDATOR (PREH-duh-tur)—an animal that hunts and eats other animals

PREY (pray)—animals that are hunted and eaten by other animals

PUP—a baby fox

Hot sun

rising over the desert

Just before dawn, a kit fox pads quietly across the dry ground. She spies a kangaroo rat beneath a cactus. The fox springs—and catches her pups' next meal! She is lucky. The time for hunting has nearly ended. Sunbeams are flickering over the landscape as the sun rises. *Chuh-chuh-chuh-chuh-chuh!* The rattling call of a cactus wren breaks the silence. The fox heads for her den as another day in the desert begins.

Wind-sculpted sand dunes bake beneath a blazing sun (above). Most North American deserts are home to many kinds of living things (right).

Does the word *desert* make you think of a hot wasteland of sand? Is it a place where almost nothing lives or grows? A few deserts are like that. But most have more stones than sand. And many deserts are full of life.

Deserts are the driest places on Earth. They are found where rain is scarce and the air is very dry. In western North America, deserts stretch from Idaho south into Mexico. The largest are the Great Basin, Mojave, Sonoran, and Chihuahuan Deserts.

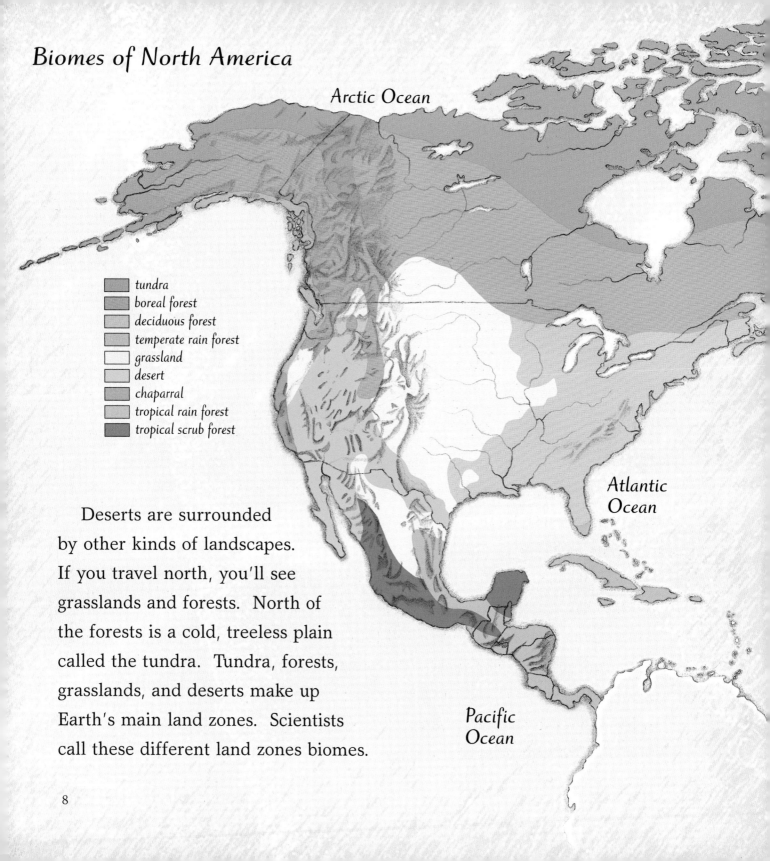

Biomes of North America

Arctic Ocean

- tundra
- boreal forest
- deciduous forest
- temperate rain forest
- grassland
- desert
- chaparral
- tropical rain forest
- tropical scrub forest

Atlantic Ocean

Pacific Ocean

Deserts are surrounded by other kinds of landscapes. If you travel north, you'll see grasslands and forests. North of the forests is a cold, treeless plain called the tundra. Tundra, forests, grasslands, and deserts make up Earth's main land zones. Scientists call these different land zones biomes.

8

Each biome has a different type of climate. The climate is an area's usual pattern of weather over a long period of time.

Every biome is home to a special group of plants. The plants are well suited to living in the biome's climate and to growing in the soil found there.

Every biome is also home to a special group of animals. In one way or another, the animals depend on the plants to survive. Many of a biome's animals eat plants. Other animals eat the plant-eaters.

Desert plants are unlike plants in any other biome. They must be able to survive with very little rain.

9

All the plants and animals in a biome form a community. In that community, every living thing depends on other community members for its survival. A biome's climate, soil, plants, and animals are all connected this way.

After a wet winter, spring flowers bloom (left). After a dry winter, the same patch of desert is parched and brown (below).

Deserts have a very dry climate. They do get a little rain, but it doesn't come regularly. One storm might drench a desert with several inches of rain in just a few hours. It might not rain again for months—even years.

Most cold deserts have few plants (below). Temperatures soar in a hot desert as the sun climbs high in the sky (right).

Some deserts are cold, but most are hot. During the day, hot deserts are the hottest places on Earth. Clouds are rare in desert skies. There is nothing to block the sun's scorching rays. But when the sun goes down, deserts cool off quickly. Nighttime temperatures can be freezing cold.

It's hard to imagine that anything could live in such a harsh place. Yet most deserts are home to many living things. Let's take a walk in the desert and see what life is like here in early summer.

The landscape glows in the morning sun. You're in the middle of a rocky plain full of strange-looking plants. Many are cactus plants, or cacti. Most cacti don't have leaves. They have thick, green stems covered with sharp spines. The spines protect cacti from being eaten by desert animals. They also shade the stems from the sun.

Short and squat or tall and branched, cacti are covered with spines.

Some cactus spines
are straight. Others
have tips that curve
like fishhooks.

barrel
cactus
spines

saguaro
cactus
spines

These barrel cacti look
like stubby fingers
pushing up through
the soil.

15

Some cacti have so
many spines, it's hard
to see the green stem
underneath (left).
A cholla bristles with
needle-sharp
spines (below).

Cacti come in many shapes
and sizes. At your feet are tiny
round cacti. They look like
pincushions. Next to them are
pancake-shaped prickly pears.
Chubby barrel cacti dot the
landscape. They grow about
knee-high. Chollas are taller,
with many spiny branches.
Towering over everything are
giant saguaros. They can grow
as tall as a telephone pole.

60 years old

Saguaro cacti grow very slowly. But they may live for 200 years.

10 years old

Saguaros grow taller than any other kind of cactus. A saguaro with many branches, or arms, could be over a century old.

17

The shallow roots of a barrel cactus can soak up rain as soon as it hits the ground.

Cacti store water inside their fleshy, waxy stems (above right).

Bend down and pick up a handful of soil. It's so pebbly and dry it trickles through your fingers. Desert soil contains many things that plants need to grow. But after a rain, it dries out very fast. Desert plants must be able to soak up rainwater quickly. They must save every precious drop.

Many cacti have roots that spread out just under the soil's surface. When it rains, the roots soak up the water before the soil dries out. The water is stored in a cactus's thick, fleshy stem. A waxy coating on the outside of the stem keeps the water in.

Cacti aren't the only desert plants. Creosote bushes and mesquite trees grow here, too. Both have tiny, leathery leaves. Small leaves lose less water in dry desert air than larger leaves would.

A mesquite tree's long roots tunnel deep underground to reach hidden water.

A spring thunderstorm soaked the desert a few weeks ago. The heavy rain woke millions of sleeping seeds. Everywhere you look, poppies, daisies, snapdragons, and other wildflowers bloom. Their bright blossoms of red, yellow, orange, and purple dance in the breeze. But in another week or two, the flowers will wither and die. Their seeds will fall to the ground. There the seeds will wait—maybe for a year or more—until heavy rains come again.

Thousands of poppies bloom on a desert hillside (left). Spring wildflowers make a colorful carpet around different kinds of cacti (above left).

21

A cluster of beavertail cacti burst into bloom (left).
A broad-billed hummingbird sips sweet nectar
from a desert wildflower (below).

Many of the cacti are blooming, too. Bright, waxy flowers sprout from their tops and branches. Hear that buzzing and humming? Cactus flowers and wildflowers attract bees, butterflies, and wasps. Jewel-colored hummingbirds stop in midair to dip their long bills into the blossoms. All these animals drink the sweet nectar that the flowers make.

22

Inside the flowers are tiny, yellow grains called pollen. Pollen sticks to animals as they sip nectar. As the animals flit from flower to flower, they spread pollen from one plant to another. This process is called pollination. When plants are pollinated, they can make fruits and seeds. From seeds, new plants will grow.

Covered with pollen, a bee collects nectar from a cactus flower.

A mother desert tortoise lays her eggs in sandy soil. The sun warms the eggs until they hatch.

Desert plants provide many animals with food and water. Here comes a desert tortoise. It shuffles slowly along and stops often to rest. The tortoise stretches its long neck to nibble a wildflower. Tortoises rarely drink. They get nearly all the water they need from the plants they eat.

A desert tortoise bulldozes its way through a patch of blooming owl clover.

Cacti also provide homes for desert animals. Halfway down a nearby saguaro's thick stem, a Gila woodpecker pecks a hole in the juicy flesh. It is making a nest for its eggs. Woodpeckers have nested in this cactus for many years, so they've made many holes in it.

A Gila woodpecker pecks at the entrance to its saguaro nest.

Elf owls are the smallest owls in the world. They are about the size of sparrows.

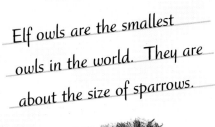

A wood rat's nest (above right) looks like a big pile of sticks.

Other creatures have moved into some of the old woodpecker holes. A pair of flycatchers lives in one. Another is home to a hive of honeybees. And peeking out of still another hole is an elf owl. It has white eyebrows and fierce yellow eyes.

Not far from the saguaro, you see a very different kind of desert home. Jammed between a dead cactus and a fallen tree is a huge mound of tangled twigs. It's the nest of a wood rat.

A wood rat nibbles on the sweet fruit of a prickly pear cactus.

Wood rats are also called pack rats. They use anything they can find to build enormous nests. A wood rat's nest might be made of sticks, rocks, leaves, cactus spines, or even bones. It may be as tall as a person and just as wide. The nest protects the wood rat from foxes, hawks, and other predators. It is also a cool place to hide from the hot sun.

Nose twitching, a wood rat sniffs the air to check for danger.

A painted grasshopper uses its long legs to hop from plant to plant—and to escape being eaten.

Ants carry seeds across the dry, pebbly desert ground (above right).

Many desert animals are nocturnal. They are active only at night, when it is cooler. Nocturnal desert-dwellers spend their days in burrows, dens, and other sheltered places. The kangaroo rat and the kit fox are nocturnal. They stay underground until the sun goes down.

But some desert animals are active during the day. Insects are on the move everywhere. Columns of ants march across the ground. Colorful beetles crawl up and down stems. Grasshoppers spring from leaf to leaf. Insect-eating spiders are busy, too. They spin silken webs among cactus spines.

The sun has climbed higher in the clear blue sky. Can you feel the heat? Desert lizards don't seem to mind. Their tough, scaly skin seals water inside their bodies and keeps them from drying out. Lizards rest on rocks, hunt insects, and cling to cactus stems. In one small patch of desert, you could see tiny skinks, chunky chuckwallas, spiny horned lizards, and lumbering Gila monsters.

A horned lizard's spiny scales are a good defense against desert predators.

A chuckwalla atop a prickly perch soaks up the sun.

A roadrunner's feet have two toes that point forward and two that point backward. This shape helps the bird grip the ground when it runs.

With long legs and a slim body, the zebra-tailed lizard *(above right)* is built for speed.

Suddenly, something streaks across your path. It's a speedy lizard, and right on its heels is a roadrunner. Roadrunners can fly. But these desert birds prefer to run after lizards and the other small animals they hunt.

Roadrunners have long, strong legs. They can run as fast as many lizards can. In fact, this time the bird is faster. The roadrunner catches the lizard by its tail and swallows it in one gulp.

A roadrunner snares dinner in its sturdy beak.

Desert jackrabbits have longer ears than rabbits from other biomes. Long ears release heat and help jackrabbits stay cool.

cottontail rabbit

jackrabbit

A black-tailed jackrabbit dines on tender leaves
(above right).

Nearby, a jackrabbit looks for plants to nibble. Jackrabbits are even faster than roadrunners. They can outrun almost everything in the desert. They can even outrun coyotes—most of the time!

Coyotes eat rabbits when they can catch them. But they will eat just about anything, from birds and lizards to berries. To find underground water, they dig holes in dry streambeds. Coyotes can survive almost anywhere.

By noon, even the coyotes are panting. It's well over 100 degrees. The sun is a fireball overhead. Nearly all the daytime animals move into the shade of rocks and cacti during the hottest part of the day.

A coyote slips quietly among bushes and rocks as it hunts.

A mother scorpion carries her babies around on her back until they can survive on their own.

Take a tip from the animals. Find a place out of the sun to rest. Just be careful where you sit. Scorpions often lurk in crevices or under rocks during the day. A scorpion's tail has a stinger filled with poison. Few kinds of scorpions can kill a person. But the sting of any scorpion is very painful.

A scorpion uses its large pincers to catch spiders and other small prey. Its stinger is used mostly for defense.

A rattlesnake's rattle is made up of a row of large, dry scales.

Watch out for hiding rattlesnakes and coral snakes, too. Their poison is deadly. You don't want to get within striking distance of either one.

Heat waves shimmer above the landscape. The leaves of the mesquite trees curl up. Curled leaves lose less water to the hot, dry air. The desert is very quiet. Most of the birds are silent. They seem to be waiting for the sun's fierce heat to fade.

Coiled like a spring, a diamondback rattlesnake is ready to strike (above left).

*The sun slips below
the horizon as the
desert night begins.*

Gradually, the sun moves lower in the sky. As
shadows grow longer, the temperature starts to drop.
Desert birds begin to sing again. At sunset, coyotes
call to each other, barking and yelping. They join
voices in an eerie, wailing song.

The hot desert day is over. The cool night is
about to begin. Birds, lizards, and other daytime
animals retreat to snug nests and safe hiding places.
There they will sleep the night away. As darkness
falls, the nocturnal animals begin to stir.

Giant desert centipedes may grow longer than your hand.

Tarantulas (above right) are some of the largest spiders in the world.

Snakes slither into the open. They are ready to track down rats, rabbits, and birds that nest on the ground. Scorpions scuttle around. They search for crickets, spiders, and small, sleeping lizards. Many-legged centipedes crawl out from nooks and crannies to hunt insects.

Hairy tarantulas creep out of holes in the ground. They look scary. But they are dangerous only to the insects and other small creatures they eat.

Bats flutter out of caves. They look like dark shadows against the night sky. Some seek the sweet nectar of cactus flowers. Others hunt for flying insects.

A lesser long-nosed bat flies in to sip nectar from a saguaro flower.

Constantly alert for danger, a kangaroo rat stuffs its cheek pouches with seeds.

An elf owl whistles softly as it flies out from its saguaro hotel. It glides silently through the cool night air. The owl dives to the ground to catch a small snake in its sharp claws.

Up from their burrows come kangaroo rats. All night they bound around on long hind legs, noses twitching, searching for seeds. Wood rats also leave their nests to look for food. Kit foxes quietly stalk rats and mice, and maybe a sleeping roadrunner, too.

A peccary uses its long, sharp front teeth, or tusks, to cut roots.

Wait—hear that? Soft grunting sounds are coming from a clump of creosote bushes. There's a strong musky odor in the air, too. Peccaries are near. Peccaries are piglike animals with coarse, bristly hair.

Peccaries are also called by their Spanish name, javelina.

A mother peccary watches over her babies. If danger threatens, the young will hide between her legs.

During the day, peccaries sleep in the shade. But at night, they travel in noisy groups. They poke the dry soil with their long snouts, eating roots and tender plants. One of their favorite foods is prickly pear cactus. Peccaries don't seem to mind the prickly pear's sharp spines.

A bobcat passed by here, leaving its footprint in the sandy desert soil.

The scent of peccaries can attract large desert hunters. Bobcats and mountain lions hide in the shadows, waiting for animals to pass by. Then, in a flash, they spring out and pounce on their prey.

Sleek and powerful, a mountain lion begins its nightly search for food.

On cold nights, desert birds stay warm by fluffing up their feathers.

As the hours pass, the cool night air turns cold. The temperature may drop 60 degrees or more between sunset and sunrise. The fur coats of foxes, bobcats, and rats protect them from the cold. Owls have fluffy feathers to keep them warm.

All night long, the desert is a busy place. It is full of slithering, rustling, whispering sounds as animals move about. By the light of the stars and the moon, they fly and hop and run and pounce.

At dawn, the branches of a Joshua tree stand out against the glowing sky.

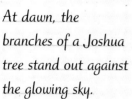

Eventually, the rosy glow of dawn lights up the
eastern sky. Owls and bats return to their roosts.
Kit foxes and kangaroo rats retreat to underground
burrows. Snakes and scorpions go back into hiding,
too. And when the cactus wren calls out at sunrise,
the cycle of life in the desert begins all over again.

*Perched on a cholla,
a cactus wren
welcomes a new day
in the desert.*

for further
Information
about the Desert

Books

Arnold, Caroline. *Bobcats.* Minneapolis: Lerner Publications Company, 1997.

Arnold, Caroline. *Fox.* New York: Morrow Junior Books, 1996.

Arnold, Caroline. *Watching Desert Wildlife.* Minneapolis: Carolrhoda Books, 1994.

Baylor, Byrd. *Desert Voices.* New York: Simon and Schuster, 1993.

Flanagan, Alice K. *Desert Birds.* New York: Children's Press, 1996.

Rauzon, Mark J. *Hummingbirds.* New York: Franklin Watts, 1997.

Ricciuti, Edward R. *What on Earth Is a Chuckwalla?* Woodbridge, CT: Blackbirch Press, 1994.

Souza, D. M. *Catch Me if You Can: A Book about Lizards.* Minneapolis: Carolrhoda Books, 1992.

Storad, Conrad J. *Saguaro Cactus.* Minneapolis: Lerner Publications Company, 1994.

Storad, Conrad J. *Scorpions.* Minneapolis: Lerner Publications Company, 1995.

Storad, Conrad J. *Tarantulas.* Minneapolis: Lerner Publications Company, 1998.

Stuart, Dee. *Bats: Mysterious Flyers of the Night.* Minneapolis: Carolrhoda Books, 1994.

Websites

Desert USA: Desert Life in the American Southwest
< http://www.desertusa.com/life.html >

The rocks, plants, animals, and people of the desert are pictured and described on this site. Viewers can also study maps of North American deserts.

The National Park Service: Mojave National Preserve
< http://www.nps.gov/moja/home.htm >

View photos of Mojave Desert plants and animals, read about how they live, or follow the kids' link to read a story about the desert.

Sonoran Desert Natural History
< http://www.desertmuseum.org /desert/sonora.html >

Part of the website of the Arizona-Sonora Desert Museum, these pages describe the life of the Sonoran Desert. The "Info for Kids" page has information about birds, reptiles, plants, and much more.

What's It Like Where You Live? Desert Page
< http://mbgnet.mobot.org/sets/desert /index.htm >

This site, part of the Evergreen Project, features pages about weather in the desert, plant and animal life, and a student's visit to a desert.

Photo Acknowledgments

The photographs in this book are reproduced courtesy of: © John D. Cunningham/Visuals Unlimited, pp. 4–5; © Tom Bean, pp. 6, 7, 11 (both), 15, 21, 45; © Steve Warble/Mountain Magic, pp. 9, 13, 16 (bottom), 22 (left); © Link/Visuals Unlimited, pp. 10, 28; © Brian A. Vikander, p. 12; © Betty Crowell, pp. 14, 16 (top), 17, 18; © Doug Sokell/Visuals Unlimited, p. 19; © Gerald and Buff Corsi/Visuals Unlimited, p. 20; © Richard Day/Daybreak Imagery, pp. 22 (right), 25; © R. F. Ashley/Visuals Unlimited, p. 23; © Barbara Gerlach/Visuals Unlimited, pp. 24, 33; © Bayard H. Brattstrom/Visuals Unlimited, p. 26; © Rob Simpson/Visuals Unlimited, p. 27; © Hal Beral/Visuals Unlimited, p. 29; © John Gerlach/Visuals Unlimited, pp. 30, 32, 44; © Maslowski/Visuals Unlimited, p. 31; © Joe McDonald/Visuals Unlimited, pp. 34, 40, 41, 43; © Tom J. Ulrich/Visuals Unlimited, p. 35; © Bruce Clendenning/ Visuals Unlimited, pp. 36–37; © Rob and Ann Simpson/Visuals Unlimited, p. 38; © Merlin D. Tuttle, Bat Conservation International, p. 39; © Carlyn Galati/Visuals Unlimited, p 42.

Front cover photographs by © Martin G. Miller/Visuals Unlimited (foreground); © Tom Bean (background).

Index

Numbers in **bold** refer to photos and drawings.